THE LITTLE BOOK OF
Prosperity

THE LITTLE BOOK OF

Prosperity

The 12 Principles of Wealth and Abundance

CHRIS GENTRY

HAMPTON ROADS

Cover design by Kathryn Sky-Peck
Cover photograph by iStock
Interior by Timm Bryson, em em design, LLC
Typeset in Arno Pro

Hampton Roads Publishing Company, Inc.
Charlottesville, VA 22906
Distributed by Red Wheel/Weiser, LLC
www.redwheelweiser.com

Sign up for our newsletter and special offers by going to
www.redwheelweiser.com/newsletter.

ISBN: 978-1-64297-010-4
Library of Congress Cataloging-in-Publication Data available
upon request.

Printed in the United States of America
M&G
10 9 8 7 6 5 4 3 2 1

For Greg Brandenburgh, with gratitude

CONTENTS

Contents

ACKNOWLEDGMENTS

Special thanks to Greg Brandenburgh, everyone at Hampton Roads, and David Cameron Gikandi for his foreword. Thanks also go to the experts quoted in this book—each one has inspired me, and I hope this book inspires you to read and study their works. Finally, thanks to my family, friends, and every student who has attended one of my courses over the years.

FOREWORD

Warning: this little book places tremendous transformative power in your hands. When I first received it, little did I know what a rare treat it would turn out to be. It was a wake-up call for me, and I'll tell you why.

I've not only read dozens upon dozens of bestselling success and personal growth books, I have authored one myself, and I've been part of the most successful personal growth films of all time. Despite all that, I still find myself stumbling and falling many times over on the path to prosperity. Every now and then I "forget" the very things I teach, and I find myself gripped by fear, doubt, and so on. That state of being "lost" can last a while, sometimes for days. And it happens to the best of us—all of us. But what always brings me back quickly to a place of strength and sanity is hearing the words of a strong, positive, trusted advisor. This is what this book is to me. A little library of trusted advisors, carefully collected to keep us all on the path of success, prosperity, and I dare say, peace of mind. It does the job of dozens of books, short and sweet, articulating what you need for your own journey.

This is not a book for those who are afraid to hear the truth about what it takes to achieve prosperity. Nor for those who want to read long, feelgood books that take forever to get to the point. This is a book for those who need short yet powerful reminders to keep them on track. It is chock full of mind gems, or wisdom in a nutshell, that will see you through both the good times and the hard times on the journey to success.

There are quotes on goals, dreams, positivity, perseverance, and more that will connect you to the wisdom of many great beings. They will remind you of what's important. I've found shortcuts to remembering my own divine path in these pages. I hope you will, too.

—*David Cameron Gikandi*
Author of *A Happy Pocket Full of Money,*
Creative Consultant on *The Secret*

The Little Book of Prosperity

INTRODUCTION

This may look like just a small collection of quotes and ideas, from some of the world's most famous and successful men and women, but it really is something far greater than that. In reality, this book is a blueprint for a life beyond your most ambitious goals. It is no less than a primer for achieving your dreams.

Over the years, I've read hundreds of self-help books that promise success, or health, or happiness, or wealth. Out of this long list of titles, only a few of the authors and books stood out as having powerful and truly helpful ideas that I enacted in my life. I found that just a few ideas from each book would stay with me, and would continue to guide me through life's twists and turns. Many of those ideas are included in this powerful little gem. I gained great riches, and the ideas that I've now put in this book were the ones that were instrumental for me. I've extracted the portions of these great books that will give you the maximum benefit.

I noticed something else in reading all of these great books. I noticed that there were themes that seemed to stand out. Different authors might use different words to describe them, but the themes emerged and I began noticing them in the books that followed. I've organized this book according to those themes, which I call Prosperity Principles.

Each of the twelve principles, when fully embraced, can be effective in helping you on your journey to riches. When studied individually, and then combined, they can be truly life-changing. This book may be small in size, but

within its pages you can find the key to riches—
from financial success, to health, happiness, and
more.

Each of the twelve chapters opens with a
short overview of the idea, and then offers some
of the most powerful ideas from modern history's
most innovative thinkers. Some of these ideas
will be one sentence, others will be longer—but
all of them have the potential to affect your life in
positive ways.

Read through the book from cover to cover . . .
or read through the chapters that seem most ap-
plicable to your life first. Since there are twelve
principles, you might decide to study one each
month. You might even think of a challenge you
are experiencing and open the book at random to
see if the words on the page inspire you to think
in a new way, or take a new action. After you fin-
ish reading and studying the book, I encourage
you to read the works of the authors that I quote

from. A list of these are included in the Resource section at the end of the book.

I also suggest you get a journal and keep it handy as you're reading. Each of the Prosperity Principles ends with a "Now Do This" section—use the journal to do the exercises. You can also use the journal to chart your progress, write about your process, and record both your struggles and your wins. This journal will become a valuable history of your success journey, and it will inspire you for years to come.

There are a couple of things to keep in mind when you are read through the book. Many of the selections were written more than a hundred years ago, so the language may reflect that time. I chose not to update or change them, since their words are so powerful as they are. You might have to change a "he" or "him" to "she" or "her" if you are female. The principles in this book will work for whomever is reading, regardless of gender. The key is to actually do the work in the book with an open mind and an open heart, and with gusto! You'll also notice that the word "life" is sometimes spelled with a small "l" and sometimes with a capital "L". When the word is "life" (with a small "l"), I am referring specifically to your life. "Life" (with a capital "L") is meant to refer to that *thing* that is greater than us, the Universe, Spirit, God, whatever you want to call it. Rather than use those other words, I prefer to use the word "Life" because I think it inspires a positive response.

I wish for you great success, however you define it, and that this book inspires you to unleash the greatness that is inside you. Every quote here can help you take another positive step forward into the abundant life that is waiting for you.

—Chris Gentry

Goals

Most successful people will tell you that they begin their journey to success by starting with a goal. A goal is like having a Life Compass. In order to know where you are going, first you need to know where you want to go.

It's a simple idea, and yet one that is so difficult for many people. It's easy to wonder which goal to pick, or if the goal we pick is the right one. But we can't let fears or confusion stop us from picking a goal. A goal provides us with a destination to direct our thoughts and actions toward.

The experts teach us to pick a goal based on our *desires*, not our fears. Pick a goal that makes you excited, that makes you want to leap out of your bed each morning and dedicate as much time and energy toward making that goal become a reality. It's important to pick a goal that is beyond your comfort zone.

Remember—once you create a goal, and set it as your intention, then begin to pay attention. Life will start to move around you and inside you, to make that goal come true. You will receive prompts and signs from Life that your goal is happening. When you suddenly get an idea to do something, then do it! Don't be passive and think Life is going to do this all *for* you—rather, Life is going to do all of this *through* you. *You are the conduit for Life to create your good.*

As you reach your goal, you can pick another, and then another, and so on. All of the other principles in this book are here to support the goal you create. Before reading the other principles, create a goal (see the Now Do This section at the end of this chapter). Then, once you create a goal, read the other sections in this book and then go back to your goal and see if you need to adjust the goal higher or lower to fit your vision.

Do not underestimate the power of having a goal. It is the cornerstone of all prosperity teachings, and it is where you must begin. Don't tell yourself that you don't need one, or that you don't know which goal you should choose. Those thoughts come from part of you that wants to keep the status quo. You are making a new choice right here and right now. You are deciding to increase your wealth, your experience, and you are going to do what it takes to take your life to go to the next level.

If you want a different experience, you need to make different choices and take different actions. That begins here with making a goal.

The Experts on . . . Goals

Desire is God tapping at the door of your mind, trying to give you greater good.
                    —*Catherine Ponder*

I know for sure that what we dwell on is who we will become.   —*Oprah Winfrey*

If you have built castles in the air, your work need not be lost; that is where they should be. Now put the foundations under them.   —*Henry David Thoreau*

If you want to live a happy life, tie it to a goal, not to people or things.
                    —*Albert Einstein*

Clarity brings prosperity.   —*Joel Fotinos*

Whenever you want to achieve something, keep your eyes open, concentrate and make sure you know exactly what it is you want. No one can hit their target with their eyes closed. *—Paulo Coelho*

Setting goals is the first step in turning the invisible into the visible.

—Anthony Robbins

What you get by achieving your goals is not as important as what you become by achieving your goals. *—Zig Ziglar*

People with goals succeed because they know where they're going.

—Earl Nightingale

One way to keep momentum going is to have constantly greater goals.

—Michael Korda

Goals are Important

Winners in life—those one in one hundred people—are set apart from the rest of humanity by one of their most important developed traits—Positive Self-direction. They have a game plan for life.

Every winner I have ever met knows where he or she is going day by day . . . every day.

Winners are goal and role oriented. They set and get what they want—consistently.

They are self-directed on the road to fulfillment.

Fulfillment or success has been defined as the progressive realization of goals that are worthy of the individual.

—*Dr. Denis Waitley*

Write out a clear, concise statement of the amount of money you intend to acquire. Name the time limit for its acquisition. State what you intend to give in return for the money, and describe clearly the plan through which you intend to accumulate it.

Read your written statement aloud, twice daily, once just before retiring at night, and once after rising in the morning. As you read, see and feel and believe yourself already in possession of the money.

—*Napoleon Hill*

Begin with the End in Mind

"Begin with the end in mind" is based on the principle that all things are created twice. There's a mental or first creation, and a physical or second creation to all things.

Take the construction of a home, for example. You create it in every detail before you ever hammer the first nail into place. You try to get a very clear sense of what kind of house you want. If you want a family-centered home, you plan to put a family room where it would be a natural gathering place. You plan sliding doors and a patio for children to play outside. You work with ideas. You work with your mind until you get a clear image of what you want to build.

Then you reduce it to blueprint and develop constructions plans. All of this is done before the earth is touched.

You have to make sure that the blueprint, the first creation, is really what you want, that you've thought everything through. Then you put it into bricks and mortar. Each day you go to the construction shed and pull out the blueprint to get marching orders for the day. You begin with the end in mind.

—*Stephen R. Covey*

The Power of Well-Defined Goals
Well-defined goals work like magnets. They pull you in their direction. The better YOU DEFINE them, the better YOU DESCRIBE them, the harder YOU WORK on achieving them, the stronger THEY PULL.

To understand how crucial goals are, observe the vast majority who do not have any goals. Instead of designing their lives, these misguided people simply make a living. They fight every day of their lives in the war zone of economic survival, choosing existence over substance. No wonder Thoreau said, "Most people live lives of quiet desperation."

—*Jim Rohn*

Now Do This: Simple 1-, 5-, and 10-Year Goals

Goals are the most important place to start on your journey to success. You have to know where you are heading before you can get there—otherwise you might end up somewhere else! Here is a good way to begin creating some goals. Keep in mind that you will no doubt refine and expand them as you go through this book, but it's important to have a starting point.

In your journal (or on a blank sheet of paper), write down the following words, with space between each of them:

Health

Love Relationship

Family & Friends

Career/Work

Finances

Play Time

You can add or change any of these categories to reflect your life.

Now, next to each of these words, write down what your ideal scenario would be one year from today. In each category, describe what you would like to experience.

Be clear. For example, instead of saying "I'd like lots of money," state "I would like to be worth $1,000,000." Or instead of saying "I'd like to travel more," state "I'd like to travel to every country in South America."

Be succinct. It's easier to remember and concentrate on short, simple goals than on complicated goals that are difficult to grasp.

You may be closer to your ideal goal in some categories than others—and that's alright. This exercise serves as a compass for a fully-satisfied life.

Next, on a new sheet of paper, write the same list of words/categories, but this time list what you'd like to see in each category in five years.

And then on a third sheet of paper, repeat listing the categories, and write what you'd like to see in ten years.

Congratulations, these are good starting goals. Again, you can add, change, or expand them as you read through this book (especially after the next chapter). But you have just taken a very good first step!

Dreams

Dreams go hand in hand with goals. Why? Because our goals are the specific ways we make our dreams come true. In one sense, our dreams are the highest goals we have, and then we break those highest goals into bite-sized, manageable ones.

To have dreams is natural. To believe that our dreams can come true is life-in-action. Why would we be born with the ability to dream if we were not able to make them come true?

Truly, every great teacher has taught us that our dreams are necessary for direction, and to lead a joyous life. No matter your circumstances today, you can dream of a bigger and better tomorrow. Those dreams help to fuel you forward.

As we grow, our dreams may change and grow as well. This makes sense, since a dream we begin with may be much too small once we reach a higher level of success. So dream big . . . but hold on loosely to those dreams. And allow yourself to revisit them frequently, so that you can upgrade as necessary.

Remember, too, that while our rational mind plays a very important part in our lives, our rational mind is not so good at dreaming. Our rational mind always wonders "how" and "when" our dreams will come. But dreams have their own paths. Dreams come from deep inside—some even say from our soul—and they aren't tied to the constraints of the limitations of our own experience and knowledge. If we only dream from what we already know, then our dreams will be small and uninspiring. But dreams are designed by nature to be larger than our experience. Dreams are meant to expand and grow us. And of course, they can inspire us to go further than we ever thought we could. Dreams add color to our lives and help us to journey beyond our wildest expectations . . . if we follow them.

The Experts on . . . Dreams

With God all things are possible.

—*Matthew 19:26*

Go confidently in the direction of your dreams. Live the life you've imagined. As you simplify your life, the laws of the universe will be simpler.

—*Henry David Thoreau*

Every great dream begins with a dreamer. Always remember, you have within you the strength, the patience, and the passion to reach for the stars to change the world.

—Harriet Tubman

The biggest adventure you can take is to live the life of your dreams.

—Oprah Winfrey

Remember your dreams and fight for them. You must know what you want from life.   *—Paulo Coelho*

All of our dreams can come true, if we have the courage to pursue them.

—Walt Disney

I'm a dreamer. I have to dream and reach
for the stars, and if I miss a star then I grab
a handful of clouds.   *—Mike Tyson*

"No" is a word on your path to "Yes."
Don't give up too soon. Not even if well-
meaning parents, relatives, friends and
colleagues tell you to get "a real job." Your
dreams are your real job.   *—Joyce Spizer*

Why should you continue going after
your dreams? Because seeing the look
on the faces of the people who said you
couldn't . . . will be priceless. *—Kevin Ngo*

We aim above the mark to hit the mark.
                    —Ralph Waldo Emerson

Dreams Do Not Die

Sometimes, the dream we have closed our eyes to the most repeatedly is the one that looms the largest. Dreams do not die. We may not act on them, but the ember of their desire burns on. Some may cite a fear of failure as a reason for not pursuing a dream. When we are young, many of us are concerned with what others think, what effect taking a risk might have on our personal or professional life. Later in life, these concerns may not loom as large, but fears of being too old or underqualified may distract us. In the end, the reasons we ignore our dream do not matter. The dream still waits.   —*Julia Cameron*

The World Belongs to Dreamers

Challenges are good. We grow through them. We are most alive amidst danger. Papa

Wallenda—the great highwire walker—
said it so well: "Life is lived out on the
wire. The rest is just waiting." The wisest
among us—the genuine leaders—smile
in the face of adversity. They understand
that life tests the big dreamers—the pas-
sionate revolutionaries. It's almost like a
weeding-out process—only the strong
(and the best) get to live their heartsong. I
really love what Amazon.com founder Jeff
Bezos once said: "I knew that if I failed I
wouldn't regret that, but I knew the one
thing I might regret is not trying."

So I'll rise above any resistance I meet.
I'll keep my eyes on the dream. I'll stay on
message and solidly on mission. Because
this world belongs to us dreamers—you
and me. And whether we ultimately win
or not, we will have made a difference.
And that's good enough for me.

—*Robin Sharma*

Dreams Have Their Own Path

. . . leaning into a project or opportunity also means you must be willing to start without necessarily seeing the entire pathway from the beginning. You must be willing to lean into it and see how it unfolds.

Often we have a dream and because we can't see how we're going to achieve it, we are afraid to start, afraid to commit ourselves because the path is unclear and the outcome is uncertain. But leaning into it requires that you be willing to explore—to enter unknown waters, trusting that a port will appear.

Simply start, then keep taking what feel like logical next steps, and the journey will ultimately take you to where you want to go—or even someplace better.

—*Jack Canfield*

Believe in Your Dreams to
Make Them Come True

There is an oft-repeated phrase with which you must be familiar. It is, "I can dream, can't I?" But this exclamation usually has the tone of futility in it, as though the person making it had no faith that his dreams will come true.

Actually, he who dares dream and believe in his dreams is the creator, to a great extent, of his future.

You would not be a normal, average human being if you did not have hidden desires and so-called "pipe dreams." While you may not confess them to anyone, you do build air castles on occasion, seeing yourself doing something or going somewhere or having something—and you take a certain joy just imagining, for the moment, that these air castles are real. It's seldom, however, that you put the power of your own feeling and conviction behind your dreams. You've never had the faith that they could be converted into actual happening, if you took them seriously instead of fancifully.

Breathe the breath of life into your "pipe dreams" by believing in them, by maintaining your faith and your dreams, unfalteringly, come what may, and eventually, if you persevere, what once was a dream will become a glorious reality!

—*Claude M. Bristol*

Now Do This:
Illustrate Your Dreams

In the previous chapter, you wrote down a list of goals in different areas of your life, for the next year, five years, and ten years. Now, it's time to add a visual element to this process. Our minds respond to these visual representations and keep us focused on moving toward them. They are like mental magnets, helping to bring what you desire right to you.

You may have heard of dream boards, or vision boards, or even created one in the past. Dream boards are visual representations of the goals that you have. You create a collage of photos or illustrations that bring life to your ideals. You will need a stack of magazines (or images you print from the computer will work, too), a large poster board (whatever size you want), some glue, and any decorations you want to add.

There are many ways to create a dream board. The simplest way is to get a stack of magazines, flip through them quickly, and tear out pages that have photos or images or words that you instantly connect with. The key is to not spend more than a couple of seconds per page. Why? Because the key is to get your first reaction, which comes from your intuition, rather than your thinking mind. If we browse slowly, we run the risk of letting our "reasoning mind" talk us out of our dreams. "You can't afford that . . . ," our rational mind might say, or "that could never happen to me," or "I don't deserve something that nice . . . ." By doing this exercise very quickly, you bypass the critical part of the brain and end up with images and words that truly inspire and motivate you.

Once you have a small stack of photos or images or words, then begin to arrange them on your poster board. Move them around until you like the way they look, so that the collage represents your goal. Glue the images in place and then add any other decorations you wish. This is your board, so have fun and be creative.

Then, place the dream board where you will see it every day. Some people put it in their office, or in their kitchen, or even in their bedroom so they see it first thing each morning, and before they close their eyes each night. The more your mind sees the images and words on your board, the more they are imprinted in your subconscious mind, and the faster they become a reality for you.

A variation of the dream board is to use a program like Microsoft Word (or Publisher) or Pages (for the Mac), or any other similar program. Create a blank page, and then fill it with images you find through online searches, as well as headlines you create, etc. This method offers a high degree of creativity. Print out your collage and again place it where you will see it frequently.

There are also some apps and websites that will help you to create virtual dream boards, and you might want to explore those as well.

Prosperity Principle #3

Taking Action

Many people dream and talk about what they want to do. Some people might take the first step toward making it a reality, but very few people actually take more than one or two steps toward making their dream come true. Fewer still stay the course until it does.

Why is it so difficult to take action toward what we want in our lives? Many of us have the false belief that we will take action once we feel like taking action, or when the circumstances of our life are just right. But the experts tell us that in order to change our feelings or our circumstances, we must first take positive action.

By the way, procrastination is actually negative action. Delaying our good takes as much (if not more) energy than to just go ahead and do something. So it's better for us to take one simple positive action, which will break us out of the hold of inaction, and create the movement forward that we crave.

When should we do it? Today. There is always, always, always something we can do today that will create a better tomorrow.

Several of the prosperity principles are action-oriented. This is because action is key to achievement of riches of any form. You can't wish and hope your way to prosperity; it takes action taken on a consistent basis.

Think of action as the price you are willing to pay for the goal that you have. The more action you take, the more likely you are to achieve your goal. I remember one student, in a prosperity class I taught many years ago, who said he would give five whole minutes a day for his success.

Five minutes! That's it! And he was serious. He wanted the results, but he wasn't very committed to the process. And guess which student in that class complained the most? Yes, it was him, the one who was willing to give the least. Think of that student, and how miserly he was with his time in exchange for what he wanted. Now think about yourself—what are you willing to do to make your dreams come true?

The Experts on . . . Taking Action

The universe will reward you for taking risks on its behalf.   —*Shakti Gawain*

In order to demonstrate true prosperity, you must get rid of what you do not want, to make way for what you do want.

—*Catherine Ponder*

Do not wait for a change of environment before you act; get a change of environment by action.

—*Wallace D. Wattles*

If we did all the things we were capable of doing, we would literally astound ourselves.

—*Thomas Edison*

Discipline is the bridge between goals and accomplishment.   —*Jim Rohn*

When it is obvious that the goals cannot be reached, don't adjust the goals, adjust the action steps.   —*Confucius*

Start where you are. Use what you have. Do what you can.   —*Arthur Ashe*

Energy follows action. Don't wait until you feel like doing something . . . do something and see how your energy changes and increases.   —*Joel Fotinos*

Better to do something imperfectly than to do nothing flawlessly.

—*Robert H. Schuller*

Here's something to remember. Action feeds and strengthens confidence; inaction in all forms feeds fear. To fight fear, act. To increase fear—wait, put off, postpone. Build confidence. Destroy fear through action.

Now is the magic word of success. Tomorrow, next week, later, sometime, someday often as not are synonyms for the failure word, never. Lots of good dreams never come true because we say, "I'll start someday," when we should say, "I'll start now, right now."

—*David J. Schwartz, PhD*

Action Completes the Picture

We can have a well-balanced philosophy, great depth of character, and a good attitude about life, but unless we put these valuable assets to work, we may find ourselves making more excuses than progress. What we know and how we feel are important factors that affect the quality of our lives. But remember, they are merely the foundation upon which to build a better future. Completing the rest of the picture requires action.

—*Jim Rohn*

Action Starts the Flow

When you take action, you trigger all kinds of things that will inevitably carry you to success. You let those around you know that you are serious in your intention. People wake up and start paying attention.

People with similar goals become aligned with you. You begin to learn things from your experience that cannot be learned from listening to others or from reading books. You begin to get feedback about how to do it better, more efficiently, and more quickly. Things that once seemed confusing begin to become clear. Things that once appeared difficult begin to be easier. You begin to attract others who will support and encourage you. All manner of good things begin to flow in your direction once you begin to take action.

—*Jack Canfield*

Do it Now!

"Going to do it" never gets anyone anywhere, and those who rise powerfully to the top of their own mountain of success are those who first survey the path to this mountain pass and then, taking the bit of the bridle of their own lives in their teeth, race to success.

Finding ourselves, knowing what we want to do, giving ourselves a legitimate time for perfecting our ability to do then doing it—this is the law of success.

Do it now! We may have only one-tenth of one percent perfection when we start anything, but practice makes perfect, and out of the very crudest material will come a gem, polished by use into a resplendent brightness.

—*Julia Seton*

Avoid Procrastination

Avoid procrastination, for this weakens your resolve. Do not keep putting off doing the things you have chosen. Start today to take the active steps to study the course you want, to acquire more knowledge about business and finances;

to prepare for the round-the-world trip, to make the social contacts you choose, to move into the house you desire; to buy the new car. You need not worry too much about where the money will come from to pay for these things; commit yourself to a course of action, and you will discover the means to pay for it.

—*Anthony Norvell*

Now Do This: Taking Action Today

Write down on a piece of paper five actions that you could do today to help further your progress toward your goals, and to bring you success. List them one through five, and be specific about what each action is and what it will entail. Make sure to list only those actions that can be taken today.

Next, put them in order of easiest to hardest. Write down the action that seems to be the easiest or require the least effort first (#1). List the remaining four actions according to the same criteria.

Now, take action on each of these items, but start with number five (#5) first, and then work your way up the list to #1. Yes, begin with the most difficult action first, get it out of the way, and you will create tremendous energy to accomplish the other four. You may create such momentum that you will take further actions than the five you listed.

Prosperity Principle #4

Growth

Why is growth one of the twelve prosperity principles? Simply because of this truth: in order to *have* more, you must first *become* more. Most people want success to come to them without making any changes (either within or without), thinking that Life will just suddenly give them what they want while they keep the same beliefs and actions (or non-actions). Unfortunately, Life doesn't work like this.

As we grow in our thoughts and beliefs, our life will automatically reflect this growth. All the experts tell us that the journey to success is actually a journey of self-discovery. If you read the memoir or biography of any successful person, in any field, you will find that success always came as the person grew. Refusal to grow means making the choice to be frustrated, stuck, and small.

Make it a habit to try to become a better person every day of your life. Be curious and use that curiosity to always try to find ways to become more happy, more efficient, more effective, more powerful. Try new things, say "yes" to opportunities, and be grateful every day for the new adventures.

Here's what I believe about you. If you do the exercises in this book and read the words and ideas carefully and apply them in your life, you will find yourself becoming a bigger version of the you that you used to be. Your life will mirror your inner growth, and you will discover new doors opening constantly.

The Experts on . . . Growth

Everyone thinks of changing the world, but no one thinks of changing himself.

—*Leo Tolstoy*

You can render to God and humanity no greater service than to make the most of yourself. —*Wallace D. Wattles*

Here is the great secret . . . you will realize your ideal when you become exactly like your ideal, and you will realize as much of your ideal now as you develop in yourself now. —*Christian D. Larson*

Whatever makes you uncomfortable is your biggest opportunity for growth.

—*Bryant McGill*

Without continual growth and progress, such words as improvement, achievement, and success have no meaning.

—*Benjamin Franklin*

No matter how many mistakes you make or how slow you progress, you're still way ahead of everyone who isn't trying.

—*Tony Robbins*

If we don't change, we don't grow. If we don't grow, we aren't really living.

—*Gail Sheehy*

If you want something new, you have to stop doing something old.

—*Peter Drucker*

Have the courage to follow your heart and intuition. They already know what you truly want to become.   —*Steve Jobs*

One can choose to go back toward safety or forward toward growth. Growth must be chosen again and again, fear must be overcome again and again.

—*Abraham Maslow*

Grow Beyond Where You Are Now

. . . you must do ALL that you can do where you are. You can advance only by being larger than your present place; and no man is larger than his present place who leaves undone any of the work pertaining to that place.

The world is advanced only by those who more than fill their present places.

—*Wallace D. Wattles*

Obstacles Make You Stronger

All down the road of life you will meet obstacles, many of them. Time after time failure will stare you in the face, but just remember this—that there is a great lesson in every obstacle you master and in every failure which you overcome. It is a part of Nature's plan to place obstacles in your way. Every time you master one of these you become stronger and better prepared for the next one. Obstacles are nothing more or less than necessary hurdles which train you and make you fit for the great race of life!   —*Napoleon Hill*

Plan to Grow

One of my favorite personal growth quotations is from author and speaker Earl Nightingale. I came across it more than twenty years ago, and it made a profound impact on me. Nightingale said, "If a person will spend one hour a day on the same subject for five years, that person will be an expert on that subject." That quotation changed how I planned my personal growth. I started spending an hour a day, five days a week, studying leadership. Over time, that practice changed my life.

To make your growth intentional, strategic, and effective, you need to think it through and plan it well. To give you an idea, I'll share how I plan my growth: I listen to audio lessons every week. I read two books every month. I set an appointment every month (. . . with someone who can help me grow).

As you plan your strategy for growth and set aside time for it, don't forget that the more you grow, the more specific the growth should be to your needs and strengths. And any time you discover that a book, tape, or conference doesn't possess the value you'd hoped for, move on. Don't waste your time on anything of low value.

—*John C. Maxwell*

Be the Change You Wish to See

Whatever you wish there was more of, be that.

Whatever you want your relationships and friendships to be, be that.

Whatever you want the world to be, be that.

If you want there to be less fear and more love in the world, start with yourself.

If you want there to be less stress, anxiety, depression and tension in the world, start with yourself.

If you want the world to be a more peaceful place, fairer, more generous and compassionate, start with yourself.

—*Stephanie Dowrick*

Now Do This:
Finish What Is Undone

Do you remember the video game Pac-Man? In this arcade classic, you go around a maze eating up dots (while chased by a gang of ghosts), and once you gobble every dot in the maze, you move to the next level. Life works like that, too.

Another way to think of it is like this: life is like a boat that we ride in. Everything we leave undone is like a small hole in the boat. The more things that are left undone, the more holes, which means the slower we go, and we might even sink.

This exercise will help you complete what needs to be completed, so you can move forward.

On a clean sheet of paper or new page in your journal, write down that same list of categories in the "Now Do This" section of the first Prosperity Principle. In the second Prosperity Principle chapter, you added a visual element to them. Now, with this new list, I want you to write down everything that is "undone" in each category. These could be small tasks, or large ones. For instance, next to health, you might write "make appointments for annual physical, dental check-up, and eye exam . . . clean out medicine cabinet . . . join local gym."

Do this for each category. (You may want to add "home" to your list of categories as well, since there is always a list of items to do around the house/apartment.)

Now, pick one item from each category, and do those tasks today. Make that appointment, write that email/letter, make that call, clean that closet, whatever.

Your list of undone items may, on the surface, not seem to relate to your larger goals and dreams. But each item that moves from "undone" to "done" allows you to travel along your path to success a little lighter, and more easily. And you simplify your life, which allows you to concentrate on more important things . . . like your dreams!

Prosperity Principle #5

Self-Confidence

In the last chapter, you learned about the importance of personal growth in your journey toward success. As you learn and grow, you begin to develop self-confidence.

Have you ever been in the presence of someone who has a lot of self-confidence? Perhaps they seem very self-assured, or they exude a sense of personal power. People with self-confidence naturally attract more success than those who are hesitant or outwardly timid.

Self-confidence is not the same as being extroverted. You can be self-confident whether you are extroverted or introverted. Why? Because self-confidence comes from a sense of knowing yourself, who you are, and what makes you tick.

People with self-confidence don't need outward approval. In fact, the more confidence you acquire, the less you are "thrown off" by external factors.

Self-confidence doesn't mean perfection. It does mean moving forward in life with a mastery of the principles found in this book. Mastery doesn't come instantly, there is always a learning curve for each principle. So be patient with yourself, do the best you can, learn from your mistakes, and through this process you will become self-confident. And that will make you a magnet for success!

The Experts on . . . Self-Confidence

Self-confidence is the first requisite to great undertakings.   *—Samuel Johnson*

Nothing great was ever achieved without enthusiasm.   —*Ralph Waldo Emerson*

There are only two ways to live your life. One is as though nothing is a miracle. The other is as though everything is a miracle.
        —*Albert Einstein*

You have to believe in yourself when no one else does. That's what makes you a winner.
        —*Venus Williams*

Believing in yourself is a choice. It is an attitude you develop over time.
        —*Jack Canfield*

Never "for the sake of peace and quiet" deny your own experience or convictions.
        —*Dag Hammarskjöld*

Beauty begins the moment you decide to be yourself.   —*Coco Chanel*

Rich people expect to succeed. They have confidence in their abilities, they have confidence in their creativity, and they believe that should the doo-doo hit the fan, they can find another way to succeed.

—*T. Harv Ecker*

If you live off a man's compliments, you'll die from his criticism.—*Cornelius Lindsey*

With realization of one's own potential and self-confidence in one's ability, one can build a better world.

—*The Dalai Lama*

What to Do When You Have Lost Confidence

If you feel that you are defeated and have lost confidence in your ability to win, sit down, take a piece of paper and make a list, not of the factors that are against you, but of those that are for you. If you or I or anybody think constantly of the forces that seem to be against us, we will build them up into a power far beyond that which is justified. They will assume a formidable strength which they do not actually possess. But if, on the contrary, you mentally visualize and affirm and re-affirm your assets and keep your thoughts on them, emphasizing them to the fullest extent, you will rise out of any difficulty regardless of what it may be.

—*Norman Vincent Peale*

Your Moment of Truth

Make this moment the moment of truth about yourself. You have been selling yourself short all of your life. You have the opportunity to experience more environmental, physical and mental/spiritual abundance than you could use in ten lifetimes. Open up your lenses to the possibilities and alternatives available in your life. Change your attitude and your lifestyle and your many environments will change automatically. Understand your own uniqueness. Appreciate the differences in others. Relax and learn to respond positively to stress. Change for the better that which can be changed. Remove from your presence those negative influences that cannot be changed. Adapt and adjust to those negative influences that cannot be changed or removed.

—*Dr. Denis Waitley*

The Effects of Mastery

As you succeed in gaining mastery over your impulses and thoughts, you will begin to feel, growing up within you, a new and silent power, and a settled feeling of composure and strength will remain with you. Your latent powers will begin to unfold themselves, and whereas your efforts were formerly weak and ineffectual, you will now be able to work with that calm confidence that commands success. Along with this new power and strength, there will be awakened within you that interior illumination known as 'intuition,' and you will walk no longer in darkness and speculation, but in light and certainty.

And in just the measure that you alter from within, will your outlook upon life alter. As you alter your mental attitude toward others they will alter in their attitude and conduct toward you. As you rise above the lower, debilitating and destructive thought-forces, you will come in contact with the positive, strengthening and up-building currents generated by strong, pure and noble minds; your happiness will be immeasurably intensified, and you will begin to realize the joy, strength and power born only of self-mastery. This joy, strength and power will be continually radiating from you. Without any effort on your part, though you are utterly unconscious of it, strong people will be drawn toward you, influence will be put into your hands, and outward events will shape themselves in accordance with your altered thought-world.

—*James Allen*

Cultivating Greatness

Greatness is, above all else, a state of mind. You need to believe in your potential and power before you can bring them to life. You need to feel like you are extraordinary before you can become extraordinary. I call this "emotional blueprinting." To see spectacular results in your external life, you have to emotionally—viscerally—create a blueprint of your vision within your inner life.

—Robin Sharma

Now Do This: List Your Strengths

This is a very simple exercise. In your journal, or on a blank sheet of paper, write down the numbers from 1 to 10 in a row down the page. Now, next to each number, write a positive quality that you possess. For example, you may write: 1. Good at my job, 2. Well-read in U.S. History, 3. A very good tennis player, and so on. Some people have no problem writing down ten things (and can even continue the list). Others might have a more difficult time coming up with ten items, or even five. If that is the case, push yourself gently to come up with more items, no matter how small they might seem to you. If you are really stuck, ask a good friend or family member to help you. Look at this list daily, to remind yourself that you are unique and possess strengths that others look up to ... and remind yourself that you continue to improve every single day.

Gratitude

There is an old saying that says "Life loves a grateful heart." This is true because when we are grateful for something, we have a positive attitude, rather than a negative one—and when we are positive, we are open to receiving all that Life has to offer.

Think of it this way. When you walk through life with complaints, gripes, and resentment, it's like symbolically walking around with your fists closed—and closed fists aren't open to receive. However, living with gratitude as your focus, it's symbolically like you are walking through your life with your hands open, in fact, with your arms wide open. Open arms and hands symbolize that you are ready to receive more from Life.

Another way to look at it is this way: what you focus on, you get more of. If you focus on lack and limitation, you automatically experience more lack and limitation. However, if you focus on gratitude and positivity, your very experience changes for the better.

Why is gratitude so powerful? Because when you are in a state of gratitude, you are attuned to the best in all experiences and all people. When you live looking for the best and being thankful for what comes your way, your whole experience of life becomes more positive.

But how can we be grateful when we feel broke, stuck, or like failures? The experts tell us to find something positive about every person, every experience, and everything that we have. They tell us to be grateful for what we already have— instead of always focusing on what we lack.

Here's an example. Years ago, when my son was small, I was driving him to his preschool. As we were stopped at a red light, I looked out of the window on my right, and saw an empty lot. This lot was in serious disrepair—cracked pavement, weeds growing everywhere, graffiti and litter, everywhere. My thought was, "what a dump." A few seconds later, my son, who was sitting in the back in his child car seat, said, "Daddy, daddy, look..." In the rearview mirror I could see he was pointing at the same lot I had just judged as disgusting. "Daddy, look at that beautiful flower!" I looked again at the lot, and suddenly I saw what he was pointing at; indeed, there was a beautiful wild flower growing in the midst of the chaos and mess. I saw all of the garbage, but my son found the beauty within it.

We can do the same with our lives. Instead of focusing only on what's wrong, train yourself to find what's beautiful.

The Experts on . . . Gratitude

A grateful heart does not need something to be grateful for. One can be grateful with the same spontaneity as being happy. It simply flows forth from within and becomes a causative energy.

—*Eric Butterworth*

"Thank you" is the best prayer that anyone could say. I say that one a lot. Thank you expresses extreme gratitude, humility, understanding. —*Alice Walker*

Whatever you appreciate and give thanks for will increase in your life.

—*Sanaya Roman*

The miracle of gratitude is that it shifts your perception to such an extent that it changes the world you see.

—Dr. Robert Holden

Be thankful for what you have; you'll end up having more. If you concentrate on what you don't have, you will never, ever have enough.   *—Oprah Winfrey*

I'm utterly convinced the key to lifelong success is the regular exercise of a single emotional muscle: gratitude.

—Geoffrey James

Learn to be thankful for what you already have, while you pursue all that you want.

—Jim Rohn

He is a wise man who does not grieve for the things which he has not, but rejoices for those which he has.   *—Epictetus*

The more you recognize and express gratitude for the things you have, the more things you will have to express gratitude for.   *—Zig Ziglar*

Develop an attitude of gratitude. Say thank you to everyone you meet for everything they do for you.   *—Brian Tracy*

Practice Gratitude Daily

Practice being grateful for everything that life has blessed you with. Every day I voice my appreciation for what I have received. I say:

Today has been beautiful.

It has provided me with health of body and mind.

It has given me food and clothing.

It has brought me another day of opportunity to be of service to others.

It has given me peace of mind and freedom from all fear.

For these blessings, I am grateful.

—*Napoleon Hill*

Living Gratitude

What is the one thing that people who can fully lean into joy have in common?

Gratitude. They practice gratitude. They keep a journal, or make a note of what they're grateful for on their phones, or share it with family members.

From the day the finding about gratitude emerged from the data, our family put it into practice at the dinner table.

Now, after we sing grace (summer camp style), we each share one specific instance of gratitude with the table. It's changed us. And it's given us an invaluable window into our kids' lives and hearts.

Embodying and practicing gratitude changes everything. It is not a personal construct, it's a human construct—a unifying part of our existence—and it's the antidote to foreboding joy, plain and simple. It's allowing yourself the pleasure of accomplishment, or love, or joy—of really feeling it, of basking in it—by conjuring up gratitude for the moment and for the opportunity.

It's allowing yourself to recognize the shiver of vulnerability—that Oh, shit, I have something worth losing now feeling—and to just sit with it, and be grateful that you have something you want, in your hand, that it feels good to hold and recognize. Something as simple as starting or ending meetings with a gratitude check, when everyone shares one thing they're grateful for, can build trust and connection, serve as container-building, and give your group permission to lean into joy.

—*Brené Brown*

Gratitude Changes You

Take a moment right now to engage in the experience of gratitude. Close the book and your eyes and just feel grateful. Don't turn outward, casting about for things to give thanks for. Remember, it is not an emotional reaction to the blessings you count; it is an energy you stir up within you that is causal. Resist the temptation to indulge such thoughts as, I would be grateful if I received that promotion and raise in salary. No qualifications, no ifs or whens. Just feel grateful. Let the spirit of thanksgiving flood your whole being with its healing and warmth.

According to Plato's law, as you feel grateful, you become attractive, not only in your beauty and radiance, but in your relationships with people. More important, you release a vital energy that draws to you opportunities, employment, and a secure flow of substance. Everything begins to work in your life in an orderly and creative way. In your gratefulness of heart, you can confer prosperity upon all the many things, experiences, and people, whose performances have such a profound influence on your life. Bless the car you drive or the bus or train you ride. Bless the weather and the traffic. Bless your place of business or employment. Bless your employer and your coworkers. Bless your investments and your cash flow. Bless your home and family. Bless your friends and neighbors. Now, blessing exerts no magic power over these people, conditions, or things. In fact, it doesn't change them at all; it changes you, your thoughts and feelings, and the consciousness you project into your world.

—Eric Butterworth

Gratitude Attitude

Nothing changes attitude faster than practicing gratitude.

Thank people for everything they do for you.

Look for opportunities to express pleasure in what comes your way.

Focus on what's uplifting.

See more and more to be pleased about. Comment on that.

Monitor what you talk about. Complain less. Or not at all!

Treat strangers with real courtesy.

Treat family with real courtesy.

Practice kindness on the roads.

Wake up to all your senses: how they allow you to engage with and appreciate other people and the world around you.

Have something beautiful in every room.

Let yourself notice how much good is in the world.

—Stephanie Dowrick

Now Do This: Your Daily Gratitude List

Here is a simple practice that will have a profound effect on your life . . . if you commit to it daily for at least ninety days. It may have been a practice that you've done before, perhaps sporadically if at all, and perhaps you felt good as you did it. But committing to it for at least ninety days will bring about a sea change in your outlook, and therefore your experience.

Here's how to do it: when you wake up in the morning, make a list of at least five things you are genuinely grateful for in your journal. These may be simple things, like your bed, your house, your job, your family and friends, and your health. You may want to add experiences you remember, people who have impacted you, books or songs or movies that you love, things you've noticed in nature, or anything else that comes to mind.

Be sure to list the things that you genuinely feel grateful for, not just things you "think you have to" put on the list. If something touches your heart, put it on the list. If someone brings a smile to your face, put them on the list. You can repeat some of the items on your list day to day, or you can try to find new items each day.

As mentioned above, commit to this practice for at least ninety days. At the end of each week, take a moment to see if you notice any changes in your attitude, your experiences, and your outcomes.

If you want to turbo-charge this practice, here is a second part you can do. At night, just before you go to bed, go over your day in your mind and add to your list. This way you are framing your day, start-to-finish, with gratitude. You can even fall asleep at night thinking of things to be grateful for.

Think for a moment—how do you think starting and ending your day in a state of gratitude would change your life? I can tell you from personal experience, it is a profound way to live, and can be a key to increasing your success in every area of your life.

Positive Self-Talk

It has been said that we become what we think about all day long. Most of us don't realize just how important it is to train our minds to think positively. We are bombarded everywhere with negativity—negative news, negative people, negative social media, and most of all, many of us practice negative self-talk. We often talk to ourselves in a way we would never even consider talking to other people. Our minds are not always peaceful, positive places for us to be in.

Everyone has an inner critic, that voice that is constantly telling ourselves that we aren't good enough, we aren't smart enough, we aren't thin enough, we aren't young enough, we aren't rich enough. That voice is constantly letting us know our short-comings.

Because we have so much negativity around and within us, it is imperative that we flood our lives with positivity. One expert said that we are exposed to seven times more negativity on a daily basis than we are positivity. I believe this. In order to counteract all of these negative influences, we must surround ourselves with as much positivity as we can.

Look for the positive everywhere you can, big or small. Write positive affirmations. Don't let other people tell you what to think. Stay the course as much of each day as possible, so that you are choosing what to think, rather than being passive and lazy in your thinking.

When we follow the advice of the experts and use positive self-talk techniques, we neutralize the negativity, and create positive experiences. Self-talk, then, becomes one of the most potent and powerful ways to create a successful life. The more you train yourself to be positive, the more you begin to see that positivity shows up in every area of your life.

The Experts on . . .
Positive Self-Talk

I expect everything I do to prosper. I enthusiastically expect success.

—Ernest Holmes

Old ideas will not create new conditions.

—Raymond Charles Barker

Optimism is the most important human trait, because it allows us to evolve our ideas, to improve our situation, and to hope for a better tomorrow.

—Seth Godin

Success is a state of mind. If you want success, start thinking of yourself as a success.
—*Dr. Joyce Brothers*

Whatever is true, whatever is honorable, whatever is just, whatever is pure, whatever is lovely, whatever is gracious … think about these things.   —*Philippians 4:8*

The greatest discovery of our generation is that human beings can alter their lives by altering their attitudes of mind. As you think, so shall you be.   —*William James*

If you hear a voice within you saying, "You are not a painter," then by all means paint, and that voice will be silenced.
—*Vincent van Gogh*

Evidence is conclusive that your self-talk has a direct bearing on your performance.
—*Zig Ziglar*

The more one meditates upon good thoughts, the better will be their world and the world at large.   —*Confucius*

Bring acceptance and compassionate self-talk. Say nice things to yourself—you're the only one listening. Tell yourself, I am doing the best I can.

—*Gabrielle Bernstein*

Make Your Mind Up to Be Happy

I have for many years endeavored to make this vital truth clear; and still people marvel when I tell them that I am happy. They imagine that my limitations weigh heavily upon my spirit, and chain me to the rock of despair. Yet, it seems to me, happiness has very little to do with the senses. If we make up our minds that this is a drab and purposeless universe, it will be that, and nothing else.

On the other hand, if we believe that the earth is ours, and that the sun and moon hang in the sky for our delight, there will be joy upon the hills and gladness in the fields because the Artist in our souls glorifies creation. Surely, it gives dignity to life to believe that we are born into this world for noble ends, and that we have a higher destiny than can be accomplished within the narrow limits of this physical life.

—*Helen Keller*

Focus on Opportunities Rather Than Obstacles

Rich people focus on what they want, while poor people focus on what they don't want. Again, the universal law states, "What you focus on expands." Because rich people focus on the opportunities in everything, opportunities abound for them. Their biggest problem is handling all the incredible money-making possibilities they see. On the other hand, because poor people focus on the obstacles in everything, obstacles abound for them and their biggest problem is handling all the incredible obstacles they see.

It's simple. Your field of focus determines what you find in life. Focus on opportunities and that's what you find. Focus on obstacles and that's what you find. When obstacles arise, handle them, then quickly refocus on your vision.

—*T. Harv Ecker*

Don't Let Others
Make Up Your Mind For You

Accurate thinking and accurate thinkers permit no one to do their thinking for them. If you're going to be an accurate thinker in the strict sense of that term, you have got to get into the habit of becoming responsible for your own thinking and your own opinions and your own ideas. It's all right to seek information from other people; get all the knowledge you can, get all the facts you can. But in the final analysis, don't let anybody make up your mind for you about anything. Reserve unto yourself the last word in your thinking. If you let others think for you, you are taking the path of least resistance.

—*Napoleon Hill*

Every Feeling Is a Result of Our Thoughts

Every negative (and positive) feeling is a direct result of thought. It's impossible to have jealous feelings without first having jealous thoughts, to have sad feelings without first having sad thoughts, to feel angry without having angry thoughts. And it's impossible to be depressed without having depressed thoughts. This seems obvious, but if it were better understood, we would all be happier and live in a happier world!

The ill effects of thought come about when we forget that "thought" is a function of our consciousness—an ability that we as human beings have. We are the producers of our own thinking. Thought is not something that happens to us, but something that we do. It comes from inside of us, not from the outside. What we think determines what we see—even though it often seems the other way around.

—*Richard Carlson, Ph.D.*

Now Do This: Turbo-Charged Affirmations

Thus far we have been creating goals, expanded by our dreams, growing, and taking actions. Now it is time for you to take that list of your goals for each area in your life, and write an affirmation that reflects each one. And then, I want you to actually live them. Here's what to do:

First, for each of the goals that you have written in your journal, write out an affirmation that aligns with that goal, and is in the positive, present tense. For instance, if your goal was to have $25,000 in your bank account, your affirmation could be: "I Now Joyously Have $25,000 Cash in My Savings Account at Acme National Bank." Yes, at the moment you write out the affirmation, it won't be accurate. But we are working on your subconscious mind, making impressions on it, and letting it work with Life to create what you envision. Write a positive affirmation for each goal. You may write more than one affirmation for each if you wish.

Second, it's time to activate these affirmations. Some people think if you write them down once, then you are done. But remember, we are constantly needing to overcome negativity with positivity, therefore you are going to turbo-charge these affirmations so they begin to create powerful effects in your life. Below is a list of different ways you can activate your set of affirmations. Pick as many of these methods as you can to do. Make sure to do at least one each and every day. Your goals are important and it is important for you treat them as your priority.

- State your affirmations out loud over and over for a minimum of ten minutes.
- Write your affirmations in your journal at least 100 times each.
- Write your affirmations on sticky notes, and place them everywhere you will see them—and each time you see them, state them (out loud if possible).
- Write the affirmations on a card and carry the card with you. Read the card multiple times each day (while waiting

in line, at a red light, during a commercial, during meditation or quiet time, on a break at work, etc.).

- Create a timer on your phone to remind you every hour (or half-hour, or even a random timer) to read your affirmations, again, out loud if possible.

- Make a commitment with a trusted friend to send each other your affirmations each day via text or email, or have a short phone call each day to repeat your affirmations to each other.

What other ways can you think of to creatively and constantly put these affirmations to work in your life?

Prosperity Principle #8

Master Mind

Here's some good news: you don't have to travel your path to success all by yourself. While you are 100 percent responsible for your own life, having a Success Partner (or partners) can help make the journey more fun, more effective, and keep you on track by holding you accountable.

What is a Success Partner? It's a person—or persons—who can help keep you focused, give you ideas and assistance, and will believe in what you have deemed your highest and greatest good. Sometimes we need someone to support us, so that we can go beyond our own limited thinking about ourselves. And of course, we can do the same for them. When we are a Success Partner to someone else, it blesses our own life immeasurably.

When two or more people come together for a positive purpose, the energy created can be amazing. Napoleon Hill wrote about this partnership in his bestselling book *Think and Grow Rich,* calling them "Master Mind partners," a term coined by Andrew Carnegie. Other success experts have used the term "Master Mind" or other terms to describe those people who can be helpers on your path. It's one of the best tools you can use on your journey to success.

At the end of this chapter you will be given instructions on how to find and create a Success Partnership that will work for you. But in the meantime, know this: every successful person I have studied has always said that they could never have achieved their goals if left to their own devices . . . the help of other people was vital to their success. Therefore, make sure to help yourself by accepting the help of others. And to increase the positive energy even more, be sure to help others as well. This creates a win-win situation that will pay dividends for years to come.

The Experts on . . .
Master Mind Partners

A dream you dream alone is only a dream. A dream you dream together is reality.

—*Yoko Ono*

Help others achieve their dreams and you will achieve yours.   —*Les Brown*

A group of brains coordinated (or connected) in a spirit of harmony will provide more thought-energy than a single brain, just as a group of electric batteries will provide more energy than a single battery.

—*Napoleon Hill*

Finding good partners is the key to success in anything: in business, in marriage and especially, in investing.

—Robert Kiyosaki

Deliberately seek the company of people who influence you to think and act on building the life you desire.

—Napoleon Hill

The next best thing to being wise oneself is to live in a circle of those who are.

—C.S. Lewis

Surround yourself only with people who are going to lift you higher.

—Oprah Winfrey

If you want to go fast, go alone. If you want to go far, go together. *—old proverb*

You become who you spend time with.
                              —*Tony Robbins*

If you want to get somewhere, walk with
the people who are headed in the same
direction.   —*Buddha*

Basics About Master Minds

The basic philosophy of a mastermind
group is that more can be achieved in
less time when people work together. A
mastermind group is made up of people
who come together on a regular basis—
weekly, biweekly, or monthly—to share
ideas, thoughts, information, feedback,
and resources. By getting the perspective,
knowledge, experience, and resources of
the others in the group, not only can you
move beyond your own limited view of

the world but you can also advance your own goals and projects more quickly.

A mastermind group can be composed of people from your own industry or profession or people from a variety of walks of life. It can focus on business issues, personal issues, or both. But for a mastermind group to be powerfully effective, people must be comfortable enough with each other to tell the truth. Some of the most valuable feedback I have ever received has come from members of my mastermind group confronting me about overcommitting, selling my services too cheaply, focusing on the trivial, not delegating enough, thinking too small, and playing it safe.

—*Jack Canfield*

The Power of Success Partners/ Master Mind Partners

The "Master Mind" may be defined as: "Coordination of knowledge and effort, in a spirit of harmony, between two or more people, for the attainment of a definite purpose."

No individual may have great power without availing himself of the "Master Mind."

So you may better understand the "intangible" potentialities of power available to you, through a properly chosen "Master Mind" group, we will here explain the two characteristics of the Master Mind principle, one of which is economic in nature, and the other psychic. The economic feature is obvious. Economic advantages may be created by any person who surrounds himself with the advice, counsel, and personal cooperation of a group who are willing to lend him wholehearted aid, in a spirit of perfect harmony. This form of cooperative alliance has been the basis of nearly every great fortune. Your understanding of this great truth may definitely determine your financial status.

The psychic phase of the Master Mind principle is much more abstract, much more difficult to comprehend, because it has reference to the spiritual forces with which the human race, as a whole, is not well acquainted. You may catch a significant suggestion from this statement: "No two minds ever come together without, thereby, creating a third, invisible, intangible force which may be likened to a third mind."

—*Napoleon Hill*

Master Minds Help Get Better Results

I believe that having a Master Mind, no matter what your goal might be, is one of the most effective success habits that we can acquire. A few years ago I read a magazine article that mentioned studies show that when people join a gym with a friend, they are far more likely to a) stay committed and consistent in showing up to the gym, b) have fun and enjoy the process, and c) see greater results.

Adding Master Mind partners to your success journey will help you in a similar way. With a Master Mind in action in your life, you'll be more apt to be committed and consistent, you'll probably have more fun, and because of these, you'll no doubt see more results as well.

—*Joel Fotinos*

Surround Yourself with Positive People

When you are considering an opportunity, negotiating a complex problem, or trying to generate new ideas, it can be helpful to seek out the advice of a friend or a colleague who can provide a different perspective. You can deliberately put this process to work by creating what in the coaching world is called a Mastermind Group, three to six people who meet regularly to brainstorm and support one another. Many extraordinary people are known for forming such groups. Ben Franklin, along with twelve of his most ingenious friends in Philadelphia, formed a group dedicated to self-improvement that met weekly to share books and ideas. Henry Ford formed a group of close advisors that included the inventor Thomas Edison and the management genius Harvey Firestone. More recently, Richard Branson, when he founded Virgin Music, created an idea-sharing group composed of producers, musicians, artists, and filmmakers.

There are a few things to keep in mind when forming a Mastermind Group. First, you should include people with diverse backgrounds, skill sets, and talents. The group should ideally include between four and six people. The group should meet on a regular basis—for example, biweekly or monthly. Ideally, the meetings should occur in person, although effective groups can also meet by phone. During the meeting, each member should be given an allocation of time to describe what he or she is working on and thinking about, and allow others to provide comments and suggestions.

In addition to providing a diversity of views and perspectives, an advantage of forming a Mastermind Group is that it keeps its members accountable. At each meeting, participants can describe the actions they will take and set deadlines to complete them. In doing so, they will be held accountable to those commitments.

This can be quite helpful in encouraging you to take positive actions that are in alignment with your highest priorities.

—*Ryan Babineaux, Ph.D.*
and *John Krumboltz, Ph.D.*

Now Do This:
Master Mind Partners

It's time to find some partners who can help you (and whom you can help as well). As mentioned, Napoleon Hill called these Master Mind partners (or a Master Mind group), others call them Success Partners. The idea is that each person has time and space to discuss their goals. The members are not there just to support your goals. And as I noted earlier in this chapter, helping the other members of your Master Mind group will actually help you achieve your own goals more quickly. Here are some simple ways to form your own Master Mind group:

Who Should You Invite to Your Master Mind Group?

- If you want to start a Master Mind Group, decide what you want the group for, what kind of support you need, and also what kind of support you can offer others. The people you want to invite should have the following qualities: supportive, not competitive, hungry for success, consistent, reliable, positive, etc.

- Then think of people you know in your professional network, people from business or religious organizations, like-minded people you are connected with on the internet (i.e., LinkedIn, etc.). You can invite family and friends, but it's important to choose only those who have the same motivation and interest level.

- And think of how many people you would like in your group—starting with 3 or 4 is a good place to begin. You can add more as necessary.

How should the group run?

- Pick a facilitator.
- Decide, as a group, how often you are going to meet (weekly, twice a month, or monthly).
- Set attendance requirements. Decide how many meetings people can miss in a given time before they are asked to leave the group.
- Decide how you will deal with disruptive members, such as those who talk too much or talk over others.

- Discuss the process by which you will invite new members once the group has begun.

Where should your
Master Mind Group meet?

- Pick a place that is comfortable, quiet, and fits the needs of the group. Places that might work include: a library meeting room, church or synogogue, restaurant, or a member's home (as long as you won't be interrupted). Some groups meet via Skype, Zoom, or even on a conference call.

What makes a
Master Mind Group successful?

- Have a set length of time for the meeting—such as one hour—and stick to that time.

- Don't discuss anything other than each other's goals—save discussion of anything else for after the meeting.
- Give equal discussion time to each member—don't let any member dominate the meeting.
- Discuss ways you can support each other, offer ideas, suggest resources, and strategize "next steps" each member should take before the next meeting.

These are just a few ideas to get you started. Personalize them so they fit the needs of your group.

Positivity

Is it a surprise that successful people tend to be positive people? That doesn't mean they don't see the obstacles on their path and prepare for them, that they don't encounter negative people and betrayals, or that they don't experience failures along the way. But it does mean that they don't let these things rob them of pursuing their passion, and experiencing the joy of achieving their goals.

It's easy to feel depleted by negativity. After all, it's all around us. From the television to the news, we see it constantly, 24/7. Have you ever been around people who are negative? If so, how do they affect you? Most likely, negative people drain you. Now contrast that to being around someone who is beaming with positivity; how do *they* affect you? Most of the time, you will notice that positive people fill you with energy . . . *their* energy.

Which energy do you think will help you achieve your success more quickly—positive or negative? There is no doubt that being positive will be the faster route.

How do you become positive when negativity is around you? Should you just put your head in the sand and ignore it? Absolutely not. True positivity is being able to see the circumstances around you, and not letting them stop you. In this way, you transmute negativity into positivity in your life. The ancient masters called this alchemy, turning lead into gold. The lead is the negativity around you, and the gold is what happens when you either don't let the negative stop you, or even better, when you can see through the negativity to positive outcomes. When you practice alchemy, you might suffer a "temporary defeat," but instead of letting it stop you, you choose to allow the experience to make you bolder, wiser, and more powerful.

Positivity and optimism are often acquired skills. They aren't always innate in each person, they must be learned. How do you learn to be positive? The examples below will give you ideas of how to be positive, and how to move forward when you experience a temporary defeat. Overall, you will notice that being positive isn't being "pie in the sky," it's more like choosing to see and feel and act good despite the circumstances around you. Being positive is another great tool you can use to speed up your journey to success.

The Experts on . . . Positivity

Optimism is the faith that leads to achievement; nothing can be done without hope.
—*Helen Keller*

Positive thinking is more than just a tagline. It changes the way we behave. And I firmly believe that when I am positive, it not only makes me better, but it also makes those around me better.
—*Harvey Mackay*

Like success, failure is many things to many people. With a positive mental attitude, failure is a learning experience, a rung on the ladder, a plateau at which to get your thoughts in order and prepare to try again.   —*W. Clement Stone*

Success consists of going from failure to failure without loss of enthusiasm.

—Winston Churchill

The mind is everything. What you think you become.   *—Buddha*

Whether you think you can, or think you can't, you're right.   *—Henry Ford*

Keep your thoughts positive because your thoughts become your words. Keep your words positive because your words become your behavior. Keep your behavior positive because your behavior becomes your habits. Keep your habits positive because your habits become your values. Keep your values positive because your values become your destiny.

—Mahatma Ghandi

I became successful due to several reasons.
I never gave up and I never let anyone or
anything get in my way. I use the power of
positive thinking to tackle obstacles and
challenges so they don't defeat me.

—*Lillian Vernon*

You cannot stop the waves, but you can
learn to surf.   —*Jon Kabat-Zinn*

Positive anything is better than negative
nothing.   —*Elbert Hubbard*

The Optimist Creeed

To be so strong that nothing can disturb
your peace of mind.

To talk health, happiness and prosperity
to every person you meet.

To make all your friends feel that there
is something worthwhile in them.

To look on the sunny side of everything and make your optimism come true.

To think only of the best, to work only for the best, and to expect only the best.

To be just as enthusiastic about the success of others as you are about your own.

To forget the mistakes of the past and press on to the greater achievements of the future.

To wear a cheerful expression at all times and give a smile to every living creature you meet.

To give so much time to improving yourself that you have no time to criticize others.

To be too large for worry, too noble for anger, too strong for fear, and too happy to permit the presence of trouble.

To think well of yourself and to proclaim this fact to the world, not in loud words but in great deeds.

To live in the faith that the whole world is on your side, so long as you are true to the best that is in you.

—*Christian D. Larson*

Enthusiasm Is a Form of Positivity

Enthusiasm is the dynamics of our personality. Without it, whatever abilities you may possess lie dormant. It is safe to say that all of us have more latent power than we ever learn to use. We may have knowledge, sound judgment and good reasoning facilities, but no one, not even ourselves, will know it until we learn how to put our hearts into thought and action.

One true eternal success law is enthusiasm. We cannot expect to fan anything into a raging flame of completion unless we do so from the red-hot coals of our own ambition, enthusiasm and aspiration.

Power, possession, attraction, name, fame, honor and success are all the product of a whirlwind consciousness. It is our own life stream that rushes us on past valleys, hills, and mountains to deliver our possessions to ourselves, and those who do not generate energy of enthusiasm are at one with the death of their own desires.

People who let their enthusiasm awake them in the morning instead of an alarm clock will never fail in business. The managers who let their enthusiasm carry them into an interest in their very lowest employees, to see that labor is comfortable, will never hunt for laborers, nor meet strikes or revolutions. Friends who meet their friends with interest, joy and aliveness will count their friends by the score. And the lovers who give a smile for a smile, truth for truth, hearts for a faithful heart will never die alone.

When we study the lives of great men and women, whether they are in the fields of government, business, science or the arts, the one common ingredient all of them possess is enthusiasm about their work and their lives. Enthusiasm enabled Beethoven to compose his great symphonies despite his deafness. Enthusiasm enabled Columbus to persuade Queen Isabella to finance his voyage of discovery and to keep going when it seemed impossible to succeed. Enthusiasm is the secret ingredient of success for the most successful people as well as the generator of happiness in the lives of those who possess it.

With the fire of a great enthusiasm within us we are burning, and we become then a torchbearer and a lamp to the feet of the slumbering multitude. We are success then, because we have set the law of our own life and, believing in the law, we come under the protection of the law.

—*James Allen*

Flood Your Life With Positivity

So how much joy do you need in your life? Let's look to research for some answers. In her book *Positivity: Top-Notch Research Reveals the 3-to-1 Ratio That Will Change Your Life*, Barbara Fredrickson suggests that to have a well-balanced, flourishing life, you need a minimum of three positive emotional experiences for every negative one. The positive experiences need not be a big deal—it can be something as simple as going for a walk or appreciating a cup of tea with a friend. The important thing is that positive experiences occur regularly and are at least three times more frequent than negative experiences, or

what Fredrickson calls the "3-to-1 ratio."
[She writes] A fascinating fact about people's positivity ratio is that they're subject
to a tipping point. Below a certain ratio,
people get pulled into a downward spiral fueled by negativity. Their behavior
becomes painfully predictable—even
rigid. They feel burdened—at times even
lifeless. Yet above this same ratio, people
seem to take off, drawn along an upward
spiral energized by positivity. Their behavior becomes less predictable and more
creative. They grow. They feel uplifted
and alive.

—*Ryan Babineaux, Ph.D.*
and *John Krumboltz, Ph.D.*

A Positive Mental Attitude

All riches, of whatsoever nature, begin as
a state of mind, and let us remember that
a state of mind is the one and only thing
over which any person has complete,

unchallenged right of control. It is highly significant that none of us has control over anything except the power to shape our own thoughts and the privilege of fitting them to any pattern of our choice.

Mental attitude is important because it converts the brain into the equivalent of an electromagnet that attracts the counterpart of one's dominating thoughts and purposes. It also attracts the counterpart of one's fears, worries, and doubts.

A positive mental attitude is the starting point of all riches, whether they be riches of a material nature or intangible riches. It attracts the riches of true friendship and the riches one finds in the hope of future achievement. It provides the riches one may find in Nature's handiwork, as it exists in the moonlit nights, in the stars that float out there in the heavens, in the beautiful landscapes, and in distant horizons.

—Napoleon Hill

Now Do This: Positivity

One of the quotes included in this chapter refers to the "3 to 1 ratio," which suggests that we need to fill our conscious mind with three times more positivity than the negativity that we normally absorb. So, how do you go about doing that? Here some ideas:

- Take a walk or do some form of exercise
- Minimize your intake of political news—just enough to be informed, but not too much to get depressed
- Create a playlist of positive songs you can listen to whenever you need a lift
- Minimize the amount of time you spend with negative people
- Spend more time with positive people
- Offer compliments and smiles to as many people as you are able to each day

- Read from inspirational books every day
- Learn meditation
- Eat well
- Sit up straight
- Improve your sleep
- Make decisions quickly
- Avoid procrastination
- Keep your living and work space clean and neat
- Surround yourself with beauty—artwork, flowers, etc.
- Go to museums
- Take a cooking class, or a painting class
- Garden
- Volunteer consistently
- Make a gratitude list (see chapter on gratitude)
- Add more to this list . . .

Now, choose one thing from the list above (or something you have added), and make that your positive focus for the day. If you choose "Learn meditation" for instance, download an app that will teach you meditation techniques, or read a book on meditation, or ask a friend who meditates to show you how. Make that your focus and then begin to do.

Being positive is not some banal version of being falsely happy. Positivity is a very real and valid choice you make to change the point of view in which you are living your life. The more you prioritize positivity, the more positive your life will be.

Decision

Why is decision a principle of prosperity? Because every positive experience you have first began as a decision you made. When you make positive decisions—and flex your decision-making muscle—you are taking control of how you experience your life, and how you think and act. When we don't make conscious, positive decisions, we are ceding control of our life to . . . no one. In that case, there is no captain of the ship, no navigator, no one with a compass to lead you toward your greater life experience. That's a role that can only be filled by *you*.

The first quote below states a truth that is honest and clear: indecision is actually the individual's decision to fail. By not making a decision, we are actually making a decision to limit ourselves and, ultimately, deciding to fail. Indecision is a choice for mediocrity (at best) or suffering (at worst).

Why do people either not make decisions or let others make decisions for them? Indecision is often caused by one simple thing: the fear of making a mistake. When asked why they didn't make a good, positive decision, many people will say something along the lines of "I was afraid of making a mistake." Fear of choosing something that will be criticized, fear of risking too much, fear of making a decision that will negatively impact our status quo, these are all reasons we might not make a decision. In business, that line of thinking is called "low risk, low reward." It's a fear-based way to go through life. On the one hand, making few decisions, or not making a decision, may feel like you are preserving the life you have, on the other hand, you won't be able to grow and experience an even greater life.

We are always faced with decisions. We can either choose to make powerful decisions based on what we know, what we've experienced, what our intuition says, and what is in line with our goals . . . or we can be indecisive or slow to make a decision, and run the risk of not achieving the goals and success we seek.

The Experts on . . . Decision

Indecision is actually the individual's decision to fail. Many people are indecisive all their lives.   —*Raymond Charles Barker*

Once you make a decision, the universe conspires to make it happen.
                              —*Ralph Waldo Emerson*

Don't ever make decisions based on fear. Make decisions based on hope and possibility. Make decisions based on what should happen, not what shouldn't.

—*Michelle Obama*

Nothing happens until you decide. Make a decision and watch your life move forward.

—*Oprah Winfrey*

A real decision is measured by the fact that you've taken a new action. If there's no action, you haven't truly decided.

—*Tony Robbins*

Choose to move towards what you decide to do rather than to move away from what you don't want to do. Making better decisions and changing our behaviors leads us to better outcomes. —*David C. M. Carter*

Whenever you're making an important decision, first ask if it gets you closer to your goals or further away. If the answer is closer, pull the trigger. If it's farther away, make a different choice. Conscious choice making is a critical step in making your dreams a reality.   —*Jillian Michaels*

Don't base your decisions on the advice of those who don't have to deal with the results.   —*kushandwisdom.tumblr.com*

The only person you are destined to become is the person you decide to be.
    —*Ralph Waldo Emerson*

You are the result of your past decisions. You will become and experience the result of your present decisions.
    —*Raymond Charles Barker*

Decisions Determine
Your Life Experience

Success and failure are results of the use of mind. Every success-motivated mind has been a decisive mind. Every failure-motivated mind has been an indecisive mind. Only the dreamer who acted with decision on his dream brought forth something new and valuable. It takes as much hard mental work to fail as it does to succeed. Failure is actually a success negative. It is the result of consistent negative patterns in the subconscious mind. Worry always begets indecision.

Every important event in your life has taken place because of a decision made by you or by someone else. Review some of these important times in your experience and you will note the truth of my statement. No great event happens by chance. It is caused by the decisive thinking of a person or persons. A decision alerts the subconscious energies that a sound and solid idea is being accepted by the conscious mind. Upon that acceptance, the law of consciousness acts and a new event or situation is born.

—*Raymond Charles Barker*

Decide Boldly

Make your decision boldly and stick with it. Make up your mind the work you want to follow, the money you want to make, the house you want to live in, the friends you want in your life, then after making this decision stick with it, do not vacillate and change from day to day. This bold decision will shape all the events of your future life.   —*Anthony Norvell*

Decision Is a
Magnetic Force

The world is divided into two classes of people: the "I Will-ers" and the "Should-I-or-Shouldn't-I-ers"; and this latter class includes the great majority of men and women.

How many times have you said to yourself: "Should I or shouldn't I?" More human lives have been wrecked on the shoals of indecision than from any other cause.

That something—the creative power within—cannot magnetically attract things to you unless it is magnetized by your decision.   —*Claude M. Bristol*

Failure Comes From Indecision

Accurate analysis of over 25,000 men and women who had experienced failure disclosed the fact that lack of decision was near the head of the list of the 30 major causes of failure. Procrastination, the opposite of decision, is a common enemy that practically everybody must conquer.

The majority of people who fail to accumulate money sufficient for their needs are, generally, easily influenced by the "opinions" of others. They permit the newspapers and the "gossiping" neighbors to do their "thinking" for them. If you are influenced by "opinions" when you reach decisions, you will not succeed in any undertaking, much less in that of transmuting your own desire into money.

—*Napoleon Hill*

Now Do This: Three Simple Decisions

The exercise for this chapter may look simple, but don't be fooled. It can literally change your life (if you do it!). Don't short-change yourself and your future, take time to do this exercise. It's so powerful that you may want to do it on a monthly (or even weekly) basis.

On a blank page in your journal (or on blank sheet of paper), write down your list of categories that you've been working with since the very first principle. Next to each one, write down the affirmation you created for it in the chapter on self-talk. Now, look at each affirmation, take a breath, and write down one or more decisions you could make right now about that goal. For instance, you may have written "I Now Have a Healthy and Thriving Body." You can create further affirmations that clarify your goal and affirm it even further. For this affirmation, you might write the following decisions next to it:

- I decide to drink eight glasses of water every day.
- I decide to exercise at least fifteen minutes a day.

- I decide to make an appointment with my general health practitioner.

Repeat this exercise for each and every category of your life that you have written down. Then, pick one of the decisions for each category, and make it now. One simple decision in each area of your life might seem too small to make much of an impact, but studies show that small decisions that create positive action will create major positive effects over the long term. In fact, you may actually see results quickly.

Here's another way of doing this exercise. In your journal, write down the responses that come to your mind as you ask yourself this question:

What three decisions can I make right now, that will positively impact my life...?

Again, write down whatever comes to mind. (If you wrote down more than three decisions,

circle three that you can take action on today.)
Now, at this moment, they are just ideas. Take
action on each of these three ideas, and they become reality. You'll see just how much you will
benefit from the positive results of those three
decisions.

Prosperity Principle #11

Perseverance

Ask any person who has achieved their goals what sets them apart from the many who haven't, and how do you think they will answer? Is it because they were born rich? No, many millionaires and billionaires and successful people of all types were born without financial privilege. Is it because they are smarter or more creative? No, many brilliant people or fine artists never achieved success. The answer is because they developed the ability to persevere, even through the difficulties, until they achieved their dream.

Napoleon Hill, author of the great *Think and Grow Rich,* wrote that most people who have dreams of success give up when the first hardship arrives. Very few not only endure the hardship, but turn that hardship into a lesson that helped them become better and stronger on their journey to making their dreams come true.

How do you develop perseverance, or willpower? Experts will tell you that it comes down to the simple act of taking action every day toward your goal. The more consistent you are with taking action, the more consistently you will see results. This is common sense, and yet it is so rare to see people actually taking action consistently.

So here is a tip for you: at least five days a week, take at least one meaningful action toward your goal. Consistent action will create momentum. And on those days when you feel the most resistance to action, be persistent.

Positive action creates positive results, and willpower is the ingredient that makes it all work. Don't take no for an answer. Don't let short-term resistance or temporary defeat stop you. You are on the road to success, and with perseverance, nothing and no one can stop you from getting what you want.

The Experts on . . . Perseverance

We all have dreams. But in order to make dreams come into reality, it takes an awful lot of determination, dedication, self-discipline, and effort.   —*Jesse Owens*

We have to stand up for what we believe in, even when we might not be popular for it. Honesty starts with being ourselves, authentic and true to who we are and what we believe in, and that may not always be popular, but it will always let you follow your dreams and your heart.

—*Tabatha Coffey*

Success seems to be connected with action. Successful people keep moving. They make mistakes, but they don't quit.
—*Conrad Hilton*

Patience, persistence and perspiration make an unbeatable combination for success.   —*Napoleon Hill*

Ambition is the path to success. Persistence is the vehicle you arrive in.
—*Bill Bradley*

I do not think there is any other quality so essential to success of any kind as the quality of perseverance. It overcomes almost everything, even nature.
—*John D. Rockefeller*

Success is almost totally dependent upon drive and persistence. The extra energy required to make another effort or try another approach is the secret of winning.

—*Denis Waitley*

When I thought I couldn't go on I forced myself to keep going. My success is based on persistence, not luck.   —*Estée Lauder*

A little more persistence, a little more effort, and what seemed hopeless failure may turn to glorious success.

—*Elbert Hubbard*

Many of life's failures are people who did not realize how close they were to success when they gave up.   —*Thomas Edison*

Build Stronger Fires

Persistence is an essential factor in the procedure of transmuting desire into its monetary equivalent. The basis of persistence is the power of will.

The majority of people are ready to throw their aims and purposes overboard, and give up at the first sign of opposition or misfortune. A few carry on despite all opposition until they attain their goal.

Persistence is one of the major causes of failure. Moreover, experience with thousands of people has proved that lack of persistence is a weakness common to the majority of people. It is a weakness that may be overcome by effort. The ease with which lack of persistence may be conquered will depend entirely upon the intensity of one's desire.

The starting point of all achievement is desire. Keep this constantly in mind. Weak desires bring weak results, just as a small amount of fire makes a small amount of heat. If you find yourself lacking in persistence, this weakness may be remedied by building a stronger fire under your desires.

—*Napoleon Hill*

Will Power vs. Won't Power

Change your thinking and you instantly commence to change conditions around you. Change the direction of a magnet and it changes the field around it, immediately, automatically. But if you vacillate back and forth from good to bad, you lose what you have gained and produce an unsettled, unhappy result. You must hold your magnetization on what you want until it has been received. This requires an exercise of will, a developed determination, a resolution to "follow through," to stay with your constructive thinking, your right mental picturing for as long as is necessary to enable "that something," the creative power within, to help you reach your objective.

I will . . . I will . . . I will . . . I will!

Say this to yourself, again and again, and mean it! Look in the mirror and say it. Write it down and say it. Speak it out loud to yourself when you are going about your day's activities: "I will! I will! I will! I will!" Make this resolution a part of your consciousness, build up such a strength of determination within that nothing can shake it.

[Or] are you using your won't power? Are you telling yourself, deep down underneath, that owing to past failures, it won't be any use to try? If you are, you are killing off your will power at the very start. You can't say to yourself, on the surface, "I will," when something in your inner mind is saying right back to you, "But you can't . . . you won't!"

"Won't power" is simply will power in reverse! You can get results from both, because they'll each serve you infallibly, as you call upon them. But "won't power" can bring you nothing, and will power can bring you everything. So why not choose your will power?   —*Claude M. Bristol*

Cultivate Will-Power

The true path of will-cultivation is only to be found in the common everyday life of the individual, and so obvious and simple is it that the majority, looking for something complicated and mysterious, pass it by unnoticed.

A little logical thought will soon convince a man that he cannot be both weak and strong at the same time, that he cannot develop a stronger will while remaining a slave to weak indulgences, and that, therefore, the direct and only way to that great strength is to assail and conquer his weaknesses. All the means for the cultivation of the will are already at hand in the mind and life of the individual; they reside in the weak side of his character, by attacking and vanquishing which the necessary strength of will will be developed. He who has succeeded in grasping this simple, preliminary truth, will perceive that the whole science of will-cultivation is embodied in the following seven rules:

1. Break off bad habits.
2. Form good habits.

3. Give scrupulous attention to the duty of the present moment.
4. Do vigorously, and at once, whatever has to be done.
5. Live by rule.
6. Control the tongue.
7. Control the mind.

Anyone who earnestly meditates upon, and diligently practices, the above rules, will not fail to develop that purity of purpose and power of will which will enable him to successfully cope with every difficulty, and pass triumphantly through every emergency.   —*James Allen*

Tenacity Is a Choice

The number one thing wealthy people attribute their success to is tenacity. Nobody achieves great success without walking through the fire. And the difference between those who succeed and those who fail is a no-nonsense commitment to staying the course no matter how hot the fire gets. There is almost always a moment when all hell breaks loose—you lose a key client, your storeroom burns down, Starbucks moves in across the street from the coffee shop you just opened—and in these moments you have two choices: You can either say Screw it, I'm out of here, or Is that all you got, sucka? When the pain is almost too much to bear, if your mindset is weak, you will give up and blame something or someone else for your failure. If your mindset is rock solid, you will persevere.

—*Jen Sincero*

Now Do This: Perseverance

Here are two exercises you can do that will help you develop tenacity. They will seem so simple that you may not believe they could possibly have any real effect. However, do them, and you will reap the rewards ten-fold. One is to learn a simple affirmation, the other is to create a simple chart. And yet neither of these exercises will be easy to carry out. They will require your perseverance, your willpower, your tenacity. If you can do them, you will get closer and closer to your goals and dreams.

The first exercise comes from Napoleon Hill's timeless opus *Think and Grow Rich*. In the book, he suggests writing the following principle on a piece of paper:

A quitter never wins and a winner never quits.

I suggest you write that principle on sticky notes and place them where you will see them throughout the day: your bathroom mirror, your refrigerator, your bedside lamp, your computer at both home and the office, your car dashboard, and any other place where you will see it frequently. Why do this? Because it will be a constant reminder to you that no matter what happens each day, you have the choice to persevere toward your goal.

What's more, it will penetrate your mind deeper and deeper so that you develop the mindset of a winner. You will become successful because you will learn to believe that you won't quit, because you are not a quitter.

The second exercise is to create a simple chart. Make a grid with seven vertical columns, representing the days of the week, and twelve horizontal rows, representing twelve weeks, or roughly three months (similar to what's included below). This is your Perseverance Chart.

	Monday	Tuesday	Wednesday	Thursday	Friday	Saturday	Sunday
Week 1							
Week 2							
Week 3							
Week 4							
Week 5							
Week 6							
Week 7							
Week 8							
Week 9							
Week 10							
Week 11							
Week 12							

Each day, for the next twelve weeks, place an "x" in the box when you have taken an action toward your goal. That's it. It's that simple. After the first few days, you will notice that you will want to see the boxes filled, showing your commitment and tenacity toward being closer to your goal. Each day you don't have an "x" in the box, you will have a visual reminder of how you held your dream at bay that day. It will become a source of pride to see how well you commit to your goal and carry it through, even when it is difficult.

Have fun with the chart, be creative. Use colored pens/pencils to fill in the squares—perhaps your favorite color for the days you take action, and your least favorite color for the days you don't. Or leave the days you don't blank, and fill in the days you do with red hearts. Whatever inspires you to use the chart to motivate you to move forward, day by day. Let this be a visual representation of your success!

Giving Back

How can giving back, or giving to others bring you success?

That's the first question that might come to mind as you see this as one of the success principles in the book. In fact, although it is the last of the principles we'll cover in this book, it might be the principle that you will want to begin with. It is powerful enough that many successful people will tell you it is the most important principle for true success. It's the one principle that provides context for all of the other ones.

What does "giving back" mean? Giving back means taking from your bounty and giving it to other people who inspire you, who are in need, or who can use it to create positive change.

What is the best way to give back? The first thing most people think about giving is money, usually to charities, religious groups, or even homeless people. But you will discover that while giving money is wonderful, giving of yourself and your time can be even more potent.

The key to giving is to not just do it once and feel like you did your share. Rather, it's like a muscle. You don't just exercise a muscle once and expect to see amazing results. The same is true for giving. You must exercise your giving muscle every day, in a myriad of ways, and then you'll begin to reap the benefits.

The interesting thing about giving back is that there are several outcomes once you start doing it on a consistent basis.

First, you notice that it feels good. You already know that it feels good to give something of value (material or emotional) to another person. That feeling grows exponentially the more you give. In fact, people often begin to give reluctantly, and then notice how good they feel as a result, and begin to find ways to give more and more, to as many people as possible.

Second, you will notice that your generosity creates good will. You are literally making the world a better place. That means that your giving will ripple out in ways you can't even imagine, to more people than you realize. Your giving can inspire others to give. Your giving can change the course of someone's life. Your giving can make the difference if someone eats or not that day. In turn, those people will have a better experience, and that positive domino effect will continue forward.

Third, you will also notice that the more you give, the more you also receive. For some people, this is actually the main motivation for giving. We hear the words "as you give, so shall you receive," and then focus more on the "receiving" than the giving. And yet, it is true. When you give, you will notice that Life gives back. Not always in the way we expect, but if you pay very close attention, you will see blessings in many, many ways.

Whatever your motivation, begin giving back today, and enter the virtuous cycle of giving and receiving.

The Experts on . . . *Giving Back*

You cannot outgive God.

—*Ralph Waldo Emerson*

Giving is the highest level of living.

—*John C. Maxwell*

From what we get, we can make a living; what we give, however, makes a life.

—*Winston Churchill*

To do more for the world than the world does for you—that is success.

—*Henry Ford*

Only by giving are you able to receive more than you already have. —*Jim Rohn*

Success is finding satisfaction in giving a little more than you take.

—*Christopher Reeve*

If you can't feed a hundred people, then feed just one. —*Mother Teresa*

Pretend that every single person you meet has a sign around his or her neck that says, "Make me feel important." Not only will you succeed in sales, you will succeed in life. —*Mary Kay Ash*

You cannot do a kindness too soon, for you never know how soon it will be too late.   —*Ralph Waldo Emerson*

The best thing to do with the best things in life is to give them away.

—*Dorothy Day*

Give Where You Are

It may be easy for people to find reasons not to give. But it's just as easy to find good reasons to give. You just need to look for them. Go out of your way to find reasons to give. Look for a compelling cause. Find an urgent need. Look for a group that is making an impact. Seek out leaders you know and believe in. Give to organizations you respect and trust. They're all around you; you just need to make it a priority.

People in need of help are all around you. You don't need to go halfway around the world or send a check overseas to help and serve others, although there's nothing wrong with doing those things. But there are plenty of people closer to home who can benefit from what you have to offer—people in your own town, your own neighborhood, even your own home. Being generous means keeping your eyes open for opportunities to give to everyone, whether it's through mentoring a colleague, feeding a homeless person, sharing your faith with a friend, or spending time with your kids. Civil rights leader Martin Luther King, Jr., said, "Life's most persistent and urgent question is, What are we doing for others?" How you answer that question is a measure of your generosity. And the more generous you are, the greater your opportunity to do something significant for others.

—*John C. Maxwell*

Greatness Requires Service

We may become wealthy, very wealthy in the sense of acquiring money. We may become billionaires by working for it directly. But very common people have done that. Indeed, many of a low type have done it. We now have sense enough not to call these great people. Careful analysis will show, in every case, that greatness in a man or woman requires service to others. The one who is working for greatness alone is the one who ordinarily never achieves it.

One of the great laws of life is giving—we term it "service." Service for others is just as essential to our real happiness and to our highest welfare as is our work for our own individual welfare. We do not live for ourselves alone. No one can. The Order of the Universe has been written from time immemorial against it.

There is no one who has ever found happiness by striving for it directly. It never has and it never can come that way. Why? Simply because the very laws of the universe are against it.

It is the one who has mind and heart centered on accomplishing the thing that is of service who may someday be elevated by the silent vote to the position of greatness. So, there is no such thing as finding happiness by seeking for it directly. It comes always through the operation of a great and universally established law—by the sympathy, the care, the consideration we render to others.

—*Ralph Waldo Trine*

Takers vs. Givers

The takers are the people who believe that their lives will always be the total of what they can get from the world. They are always thinking get, get, get. They plan and scheme ways to get what they want in money, in love, in happiness, and in all kinds of good. No matter that they may be applying metaphysical techniques, they still may very well be takers. But whatever may be their spiritual ideals or lack of any, no matter what they take, they can never know peace or security or fulfillment.

The givers, on the other hand, are convinced that life is a giving process. Thus their subtle motivation in all their ways is to give themselves away, in love, in service, and in all the many helpful ways they can invest themselves. They are always secure,

for they intuitively know that their good
flows from within.

—*Eric Butterworth*

There Are Many Ways to Give

Giving to others is essential to happiness.
It is beautifully achieved in these and a
thousand other (free) ways.

Allowing yourself to be fully present

Accepting people as they are

Being courteous

Giving more of your time, interest and
   concern than is necessary

Taking an interest in others' interests

Valuing qualities more than
   achievements

Listening without judging

Paying attention to what someone needs
   and not what you think they need

Refusing to pass on hurtful gossip

Taking about what's positive, stimulat-
ing, uplifting

Giving the benefit of the doubt

Accepting difference—and enjoying it

Letting past hurts go

Not blaming

Choosing cheerfulness

Letting mistakes go

Resisting all temptation to sulk, stone-
wall, "punish"

Not keeping accounts about what you
have given or what you are owed

Receiving gracefully

Limiting your demands

Giving all the time you have promised—
and more

Paying attention to whoever might be
feeling left out

Praising, encouraging, rejoicing

Valuing your strength and talents—and
sharing them

What do you want most? Practice giving
that.

—*Stephanie Dowrick*

Now Do This: Giving Back

You may find this to be the single most important
and beneficial suggestion in the entire book. Certainly if you take this action to heart and actually
do it everyday, my guess is that you will find yourself experiencing more joy, more peace, and more
abundance than ever before. It certainly is what
I experienced when I began to put the power of
giving back to work in my life.

I've suggested you do several things when
you wake up, including keeping a journal and
making a daily gratitude list. While you do those
things, think to yourself:

Today I choose to be generous to everyone I
meet.

Close your eyes as you say that to yourself several times, so that you can feel it. Imagine for a moment how good it is to offer generosity to others, whether it is financial or otherwise (refer to the list above, written by Stephanie Dowrick, for other ideas).

Now, each person you meet throughout the day, think to yourself, *how can I best give to them?* And then give that thing to them. It might be a smile to someone who seems to be having a hard day. It might be buying some food for a homeless person you see on the street. It might be giving your complete nonjudgmental attention to someone who needs to share something happening to them. It might be a hug, or help with a chore or a project, or countless other ways. Giving doesn't always mean large sums of money, time, or effort. Sometimes it just means being kind and looking people in the eye.

On the other hand, while there are many ways to give that don't involve money, I think it's important to give back financially as well. Give to people or organizations that inspire you, that give to others, that will create a positive impact in the world. I'm not suggesting you give all of what you have, or go into debt or lack to give to others. I am suggesting that you look at your budget each week or month, and choose an amount that feels good to give to something that is meaningful to you. Some people develop a practice of regularly giving 3 percent, 5 percent, or even 10 percent of what they earn to those who are less fortunate. You decide what you feel comfortable with, and then do it consistently.

Try this, and see for yourself how you not only experience more success by giving back, but more importantly you will feel like a success. If you practice only one of the powerful principles in this book, make it this one!

AFTERWORD

Congratulations! You have started your journey to more prosperity, and I hope you are loving each step on the path. It can be difficult to stay the course, but you now have all the tools you need to go to places you have only dreamed of, and beyond. Now, it's up to you to do the work, take the actions, stay positive, and be consistent.

I think your completing this book deserves a little reward. Here is a certificate you can complete to make it official.

I, _____, have completed

The Little Book of Prosperity!

I now choose to:

Always have a goal

Dream big

Take positive actions daily

Always learn and grow

Step forward with confidence

Be grateful daily for all of my blessings

Use positive self-talk

Create a Master Mind group

See the positive in all situations and people

Make wise decisions

Be consistent and persevere

Give back to others

This book is just one step on my journey to riches—and I will keep moving forward!

Signed _____

Date _____

RESOURCES

The material in this book came from many sources, including the authors and books listed below. Please spend some time researching and learning about each of these teachers. Avail yourself of the books, videos, workshops, and any other material you can find from these wise experts (some living, some dead, but all of them amazing).

James Allen—*As a Man Thinketh* (St. Martin's Essentials), *Mastery of Destiny* (St. Martin's Essentials), and *From Poverty to Power* (various editions available)

Ryan Babineaux, Ph.D. and John Krumboltz, PhD—*Fail Fast, Fail Often* (TarcherPerigee)

Raymond Charles Barker—*The Power of Decision* (TarcherPerigee)

Claude M. Bristol—*TNT: The Power Within You*
(various editions available)

Brené Brown—*Dare to Lead* (Random
House)

Eric Butterworth—*Spiritual Economics* (Unity
Village)

Julia Cameron—*It's Never Too Late to Begin
Again* (TarcherPerigee)

Jack Canfield—*The Success Principles* (William
Morrow)

Richard Carlson—*You Can Be Happy No Matter
What* (New World Library)

Stephen R. Covey—*The 7 Habits of Highly Effective People* (Simon & Schuster)

Stephanie Dowrick—*Choosing Happiness*
(TarcherPergiee)

T. Harv Ecker—*Secrets of the Millionaire Mind*
(HarperBusiness)

Joel Fotinos—*The Think and Grow Rich Journey*
(CreateSpace)

Napoleon Hill—*Think and Grow Rich* (St. Martin's Essentials), *The Road to Success* (TarherPerigee), *Success Habits* (St. Martin's Essentials), and *The Master Key to Riches* (various editions available)

Helen Keller—*The Story of My Life* (various editions available)

Christian D. Larson—*Your Forces and How to Use Them* (various editions available)

John C. Maxwell—*Make Today Count* (Center Street)

Anthony Norvell—*The Million Dollar Secret Hidden In Your Mind* (TarcherPerigee)

Norman Vincent Peale—*The Power of Positive Thinking* (Touchstone)

Jim Rohn—*7 Strategies for Wealth & Happiness* and *The Five Major Pieces to the Life Puzzle* (Harmony)

Julia Seton—*The Science of Success* (various editions available)

Robin Sharma—The Greatness Guide (HarperBusiness)

Jen Sincero—You Are a Badass at Making Money (Viking)

Ralph Waldo Trine—*The Winning of the Best* (various editions available)

Denis Waitley—The Psychology of Winning (Berkley)

Wallace D. Wattles—The Science of Getting Rich (St. Martin's Essentials)

ABOUT THE AUTHOR

Chris Gentry is a successful businessperson, teacher, and author. He lives in New England. He can be reached at chrisgentry@yahoo.com.